A New

Attitude

Achieving Personal and Professional Success by Keeping a Positive Mental Outlook

A NEW ATTITUDE

Achieving Personal and Professional Success by Keeping a Positive Mental Outlook

By
Marian Thomas

CAREER PRESS
3 Tice Road
P.O. Box 687
Franklin Lakes, NJ 07417
1-800-CAREER-1
201-848-0310 (NJ and outside U.S.)
Fax: 201-848-1727

A NEW ATTITUDE
Cover design by Barry Littman
Printed in the U.S.A. by Book-mart Press

To order this title, please call toll-free 1-800-CAREER-1 (NJ and Canada: 201-848-0310) to order using VISA or Master-Card, or for further information on books from Career Press.

Library of Congress Cataloging-in-Publication Data

Thomas, Marian.
    A new attitude : achieving personal and professional success by keeping a positive mental outlook / by Marian Thomas.
        p.   cm.
    Originally published: Shawnee Mission, KS : National Press Publications, c1995, in series: Productivity series (Shawnee Mission, Kan.)
    Includes index.
    ISBN 1-56414-358-9
    I. Success--Psychological aspects. 2. Success in business.
3. Attitude (Psychology)   I. Title.
    [BF637.S8T5226   1998]
    158.1--dc21   98-5751

Contents

Introduction

Whom do you truly admire or consider a role model in your company, community, family, or circle of friends? What is it about that person that makes him or her stand out above the rest? What attributes does he or she possess that you would want to emulate?

If you asked 100 different people these same questions, they might come up with 100 different answers, but chances are each and every person they named would share one common quality: a positive mental attitude.

But can something so simple actually be the secret to their success? Absolutely! Studies have shown that a positive mental attitude is very important to your success and your well-being. Although it can't guarantee immediate health and wealth, it can make your life more enjoyable and rewarding—personally as well as financially!

Introduction

How do you get your attitude working for you rather than against you? Start by believing in yourself—by using positive self-talk and visualizing positive things happening to you. Learn to attack your problems head-on and continually look for the bright side in any situation. Rely on your sense of humor when the going gets tough and try to make any task fun. Finally, don't forget to reward yourself for a job well done.

This handbook will show you how to take these steps toward achieving a positive mental attitude and, more importantly, what you really want out of life. It also will explain how you can turn around a bad attitude, cope with an ever-changing work environment, create job satisfaction, conquer stress, and deal with all kinds of people.

Now, begin reading by putting a smile on your face. Remember, a positive mental attitude is your first step toward accomplishing anything.

Chapter 1

The Importance of a Positive Mental Attitude

Experts estimate that success is 80 percent attitude and 20 percent aptitude. A positive mental attitude can enrich your personal life, your relationships, and your career. At work, a positive outlook can mean the difference between actually enjoying what you do or simply tolerating it. It also can mean more opportunities for advancement.

Positive mental attitude and success

Over the years, several studies have been conducted to determine the effect that attitude has on job performance. Martin Seligman, Ph.D., a professor of psychology at the University of Pennsylvania, examined positive mental attitude at a major life insurance company. In his findings, Seligman discovered that those agents who anticipated a positive response outsold their counterparts who had a negative outlook by 37 percent. Even individuals who had failed the standard industry entrance test, but who had high expectations, outsold the average insurance representative by 10 percent.

Pessimist vs. optimist

Generally, when things go wrong, pessimists blame themselves, whereas optimists blame outside sources. When things go right, pessimists credit luck, while optimists credit hard work. It is best to possess some aspects of each personality.

Learned response

We were all programmed to have either pessimistic or optimistic tendencies as children. Perhaps you remember receiving messages from your parents such as, "You can do it," or "Give it a try." If so, you probably possess more optimistic characteristics as an adult.

On the other hand, if you repeatedly heard comments such as, "Don't waste your time trying," or "You never do anything right," you will probably be more prone to pessimistic tendencies.

While these attitudes may have been instilled in you at an early age, they don't have to remain with you for a lifetime.

Potential problem areas

In your work, you can anticipate and handle problems better if you are aware of the areas where potential problems may arise. Some of these are:

- Relationships with your boss, co-workers, or customers.
- Your salary—how much you earn and how you get raises.
- The environment in which you work.
- Your actual job function/responsibilities.
- Technological advances.

These are just a few of the areas that can cause problems. You also may find that problems at home or in your relationships can spill over into work.

Positive mental attitude and your well-being

We spend about one-third of our lives working. Experts estimate that a whopping 60 percent of us are unhappy with our jobs.

Disliking your job, your boss, or your co-workers will eventually have a negative effect on your overall outlook on life.

Stress can be caused by a feeling of helplessness or feeling you have no control over your life. Maintaining a positive mental attitude will give you the power to accomplish those things that are important in your life.

If your unhappiness at work is chronic, you may find that:

- You have a hard time getting up in the morning.
- You require more sleep than usual.
- You are sick more often.
- You and your spouse argue more than normal.

- You have less patience with your children.
- You are unpleasant with your co-workers and/or boss.
- You are making more mistakes.
- You are overeating, drinking to excess, or participating in other self-destructive behaviors.

Making the most of work

The best way to make the most of your work situation is to find all the positive aspects of your job and focus on them. Concentrate on framing work as a factual aspect of your life. Examples of facts would be:

- I make enough money to support my family.
- My hours allow me to get my children off to school in the morning and be with them when they get home at night.

Examples of judgments and opinions would be:

- I could probably make more money elsewhere.
- My boss doesn't like me.

If the positives outweigh the negatives, make an effort to start concentrating on the positive aspects of your job now. You will soon find the situation more enjoyable.

If, on the other hand, the negatives outweigh the positives, it's time to examine the situation more closely. If you're in a rut, you can learn how to dig your way out later in this book. If there really aren't that many positive aspects about your job, you may want to consider starting a job search.

Work attitude

Record all the positive things about your job in the left column. Record all the negative things about your job in the right column. Remember to keep your list factual.

	Positive	**Negative** (Judgments & Opinions)
1.	_____	_____
2.	_____	_____
3.	_____	_____
4.	_____	_____
5.	_____	_____
6.	_____	_____
7.	_____	_____
8.	_____	_____
9.	_____	_____
10.	_____	_____
11.	_____	_____
12.	_____	_____

Refer back to this assessment as you continue to read.

Conclusion

A positive outlook at work can mean the difference between succeeding and failing, being happy and being miserable.

A New Attitude

No one is a winner all the time. But if you have a positive outlook about life, chances are you will be happier, healthier and more successful.

The difference between a winner and a loser is that when a winner fails, he starts over and tries again. A loser simply gives up.

In this book you will learn the following:

- How to develop and maintain a positive mental attitude.
- How to use a positive mental attitude to get what you want.
- How to turn a negative attitude into a positive one.
- How your attitude affects others.
- How to remain positive during times of change.
- How physical appearance affects your attitude.
- How to maintain a positive attitude even during crises.
- How to turn failure into a positive experience.
- How to deal with the fear of success.
- How to avoid feelings of inferiority.

Chapter 2

Developing and Maintaining a Positive Mental Attitude

Think of the people in your office who radiate an image of confidence and self-assurance. In reality, these individuals are no different from you. The only difference is that they have confidence in their ability to get past the setbacks in their lives and, as a result, they do.

You, too, can be confident and self-assured. All it takes is a positive mental attitude.

The theory of self-fulfilling prophecy

The self-fulfilling prophecy is a well-known theory that says the more you expect from a situation, the more you will get. In other words, if you expect to be successful, you will be successful. Similarly, if you expect to fail, you probably will.

Positive expectations about other people and optimism about life pay hefty dividends. Research on the phenomenon of self-fulfilling prophecies provides ample evidence that other people act in ways that are consistent with our expectations of them.

If we expect others to fail, they probably will. If we expect them to succeed, they probably will. Much of this has to do with how we behave toward others. Our expectations shape our own behavior, not just that of others. Optimists are also much better off than pessimists. Optimists are healthier, live longer, are more successful in their careers, and even score higher on aptitude tests.

Pessimists tend to neglect themselves and may even weaken their immune systems. It really does help us, as well as others, to look at the bright side of things.

Say, for example, you feel that you deserve a raise. If you go to your boss saying to yourself, "She'll never give me a raise. I probably haven't worked as hard as I could have the last six months," chances are you won't get the raise.

On the other hand, if you confidently walk into your boss's office thinking, "I've worked really hard these last six months. I deserve this raise," you will have a much better chance of getting one.

Self-talk

Have you talked to yourself lately? It is a key step in the process of developing a positive mental attitude.

Making positive statements to yourself such as, "It may take me longer than I originally thought, but I will get this done," or "I have worked hard and I deserve a raise," will help you achieve your goals.

Change negative self-talk into positive self-talk

Negative self-talk gets you nowhere. It can even prevent you from recognizing when there is a problem. And if you don't know there is a problem, you can't find a solution.

For example, making a statement such as, "I hate my job. I'm no good at it, and nobody likes me," is pointless. A more productive approach would be to say, "I'm not satisfied with my job. I think I will talk to personnel to see what other opportunities might be available."

Positive self-talk focuses on the fact that you have choices. It also helps to boost your mood and motivates you to do something about an unhappy situation.

Listen to yourself. Are you hearing statements such as, "I don't have a chance of getting that job. I'm sure I don't have the qualities they are looking for"?

If this sounds like you, break the pattern. The next time you say something negative, turn the sentence into a positive. For example, instead of saying, "Why try for the promotion?" say, "I will try for the promotion. My skills and experience qualify me, and I can prove it." Then go about devising a plan to prove your ability to handle the job.

Avoid using phrases such as "should have." For example, don't say, "I should have done better." A more positive approach would be to say, "I could have done better. Next time I will work harder to prepare."

Recognizing negative self-talk

Sometimes you engage in negative self-talk without even realizing it. How do you know? The following situations provide a clue.

When things don't turn out the way you plan

You may find that you are sabotaging your efforts without knowing it.

For example, let's say you find out that a job you have wanted for a long time is available in your company. You are excited about applying for it until you look at the salary, which is considerably more than you are currently making. Without being aware of it, you may begin to say things to yourself such as, "They'll never pay me that kind of money."

If you go into the interview with the attitude that you are not worth what the job pays, the interviewer will probably come to the same conclusion.

When you become too critical

If you find fault with everyone around you, you are probably involved in negative self-talk. Often, this kind of behavior is precipitated by overall unhappiness with your circumstances.

Visualize the positive

Practice makes perfect. Whether you are giving a speech or presenting your boss with an idea, practice helps you refine what you are going to say and the way you will say it. You also need to rehearse the situation in your mind. Being able to clearly visualize a positive experience will help you handle the situation with greater self-confidence and create a positive attitude.

Attack problems head-on

When a problem arises, address it immediately.

Let's look at the following example. Mary comes to work and discovers that she has forgotten to mail a letter her boss asked her to get out the day before. She decides to put off telling him about it until he is in "the right mood." She can't keep her mind on her work, which puts her further behind, and she snaps at her co-workers. By not telling him immediately, she has cast a negative shadow over her entire day and her state of mind.

If Mary had told her boss about the letter first thing in the morning, she would have gotten the unpleasant task out of the way and been able to go on with the rest of her work.

Look for the bright side

Life is full of good and bad. Because it does you no good to concentrate on the bad things, focus your energy on the good things.

For example, if you have a supportive spouse and a satisfying family life, but an unfulfilling career, focus your energy on your home life. You *do* need to examine your career and figure out what you can do to improve it, but don't waste all your time thinking about how miserable you are at work.

Turning negatives into positives

List below five negative statements you have made about yourself lately.

Negative Statements

1. _____
2. _____
3. _____
4. _____
5. _____

Now, turn your negative statements into positive statements by rewriting them here:

Positive Statements

1. _____
2. _____
3. _____
4. _____
5. _____

Think about this transition and the difference it will make by changing negative self-talk into positive self-talk.

Make a conscious effort to do this any time you catch yourself making negative statements. Carry a small index card with with you for the next three weeks. It should read **Negative Self-Talk** on one side and **Positive Self-Talk** on the other (see following example). Every time you think of a negative, write it down, but immediately change it into a positive. Continue this exercise daily. Note any trends you see.

Negative Self-Talk

1. _____
2. _____
3. _____
4. _____
5. _____

Positive Self-Talk

1. _____
2. _____
3. _____
4. _____
5. _____

Put your sense of humor to work

Generally, those people we identify as having a particularly good sense of humor have a positive outlook on life. That's because these individuals tend to find humor in life's little annoyances.

When something bad happens, think of how you will feel about it five years from now. If you think you will probably find it humorous, then try to find something funny about it now.

On the first day of her new job, Ann spilled coffee on her boss's in-basket. "How could I do something so stupid?" she asked herself at the time. She knew if her boss found out, he would think that she was incompetent and that he had made a mistake in hiring her. She was nervous and self-conscious the rest of the day and, as a result, she didn't have a very good first day on the job.

Today Ann laughs about her first-day jitters and talks about the experience openly. If she had done the same thing at the time, she would have been able to put the coffee incident behind her that moment and move on.

If we try, we can find a humorous side to many of the uncomfortable or negative situations we face every day. For example, Lynette was working on correspondence for her boss. With her mind on a family crisis, she inadvertently addressed the letter she was working on to "Kernel" Tom Smith. She left the letter on her desk and went for a cup of coffee. When she returned, two of the secretaries were standing around her desk snickering.

Her first response was embarrassment. "They must think I'm an idiot," she said to herself. But then, Lynette began to put things into perspective. At lunch she even told her co-workers what she had done.

Make an effort to begin looking for the humor in simple problems and soon it will become a habit.

One of the benefits of humor is that it doesn't allow you to take yourself too seriously. When you make a mistake, see if you can find a humorous side to it. If you can, share it with others.

Making work fun

Making your job fun will not only improve your mental attitude, but it will also make you more successful and creative.

Studies have shown that people who make an effort to have fun at work tend to be:

- More satisfied with their jobs.
- Less anxious.
- More creative.
- More highly motivated.
- Sick less often.

Fun at work can be initiated by the organization or by each individual. If your company doesn't create a fun atmosphere, then it's up to you to create your own.

Establish challenges

For example, if you are in sales, predict how many sales you will make in one day's time. Be sure to set up some kind of reward system for winning.

Turn a radio on

If it is appropriate for your work environment and your boss and co-workers don't object, music can brighten your attitude and make the day go by faster.

Develop personal relationships with your co-workers

If you feel as if you are working with friends, work is more likely to be fun.

Try to make work fun for others

Challenge co-workers to beat you in your own contests. For example, challenge them to sell more than you in a given amount of time.

Make the most of your free time

If you can get away from your work during breaks or lunch, do so. Read a book in the park, take a walk, or do some window shopping.

Accentuate the positive

Concentrate on the things you do well. If you are an excellent typist, extremely organized, and good at book-keeping, don't continually berate yourself for your poor shorthand skills. Find a way to improve your shorthand. In the meantime, congratulate yourself for your proficiency in other areas.

Verbalize positive experiences

Everyone likes to hear positive, upbeat stories. A warning: Don't overdo it. Share your successes but don't brag about them.

Reward yourself

When you accomplish a goal, reward yourself. Take a long, hot bath or go for a walk. You need to find ways to reinforce your positive accomplishments.

Be open-minded

When presented with a challenge, be open to various ways of accomplishing it. Don't waste time saying things such as, "It will never work."

Personal inventory

How you feel depends on how you look at yourself. Below list all the positive things (assets) about yourself as well as the things you feel are liabilities.

	Assets	Liabilities
1.	_____	_____
2.	_____	_____
3.	_____	_____
4.	_____	_____
5.	_____	_____
6.	_____	_____
7.	_____	_____
8.	_____	_____
9.	_____	_____
10.	_____	_____
11.	_____	_____
12.	_____	_____

When you feel negative, look at your assets list to feel better about yourself. Use the liabilities list as opportunities for self-improvement. Use this as a checking account—build your assets and reduce your liabilities through changing attitudes and behavior.

Conclusion

Research has demonstrated that negative thinking can hold you back, whereas positive thinking propels you toward success. If you have the talent, work hard and believe you can achieve your goal, you will be more likely to succeed.

Whether you go through life with a positive, upbeat outlook or a defeatist attitude is up to you. When you get up in the morning, you can either look at the world and say, "This is going to be a great day," or you can say, "This is going to be a lousy day." If you truly believe it's going to be a good day, chances are it probably will be. However, if you're convinced it's going to be a bad day, you may get what you expect.

Chapter 3

Using a Positive Mental Attitude to Get What You Want

A positive mental attitude also can be useful in helping you attain your dreams.

Following are some tips that will help you view your dreams in a positive frame of mind.

Establish goals

You can't achieve your goals if you don't know what you want.

Start small and be realistic. If you are currently a secretary, it's a little ambitious to set a goal of becoming president of the company by next year. It is not, however, too ambitious to set a goal to get out of the secretarial pool and into an assistant manager's position within three years.

Identify roadblocks

For example, have you and someone who can help you realize your goal not gotten along in the past? If so, take steps now to mend the relationship. Don't wait until it's time to talk to him about a job in his department.

Develop strategies

If your goal is to get out of the secretarial pool and into a marketing assistant's job, figure out exactly how you plan to do it.

Identify the worst that could happen

The best way to handle fear is to attack it head-on. The longer you ignore it, the worse it becomes in your mind. For example, consider what the worst possible scenario would be if you didn't get the job. What do you do then?

Set high expectations

Expectations are powerful, because they are the frames into which you fit reality. In this way, you see what you expect to see, rather than what actually may be occurring. Social psychologists have referred to this as the Pygmalion effect, which is based on a Greek myth. Pygmalion, a sculptor who carved a statue of a beautiful woman, fell in love with the statue and brought it to life by the strength of his perceptions.

When asked the question, "What is the difference between leaders and managers?" subordinates at all levels tended to answer that leaders bring out the best in us.

They prompt us to achieve even more than we originally believed possible ourselves.

Role models and leaders help us achieve in ways that lead to extraordinary achievements. Their expectations have their strongest and most powerful influence on us in times of uncertainty and turbulence.

For example, if you didn't get that job, your plan might be to find out why and then try to improve on your shortcomings.

Focus on success

Visualize in your mind what it will be like to be promoted. How will it feel? How will you dress? What will you do each day? By seeing yourself in the actual situation, you will be more likely to work toward achieving it.

Avoid negative thoughts

Figure out what the possible negatives are, find a way to avoid them or correct them and then move on.

Dress and act the part

If you want to become an assistant in the marketing department, you're going to need to fit in. Therefore, start to change your image so you look and act like a marketing assistant.

Take action

Don't sit back and wait for "the best time." The best time *is now!* So go for it!

Maintain a well-balanced life

If you pay equal attention to your family and personal life, you will find negatives easier to handle when they do come about.

Don't dwell on the past

When you learn from the past to help you succeed in the future, it's positive. When you allow the past to get in the way of your future, it's negative. Worrying about past failures is a destructive habit that can prevent you from getting what you want in the future.

Dwelling on "what could have been" makes you feel helpless. If you're not careful, it can immobilize you and prevent you from moving forward.

Don't view life as an all-or-nothing proposition

Very few situations in life are all or nothing. "If I don't get this job, I might as well give up. Nobody else will hire me." A more positive thought would be, "If I don't get this job, I will just have to try harder the next time, and maybe I'll get an even better job."

Dream list

List your dreams in the "I Want" column. Verbalize what you really want, making sure you visualize it, feel it, taste it and even smell it. After you're satisfied with what you "see" and have it recorded in your "I Want" column, determine the steps you will take to achieve it and record them in the "I Must" column. Each step taken, no matter how small, will give you the confidence to continue to the next step.

To Achieve What

	I Want	I Must
Dream #1	_____	_____
	_____	_____
	_____	_____
Dream #2	_____	_____
	_____	_____
	_____	_____
Dream #3	_____	_____
	_____	_____
	_____	_____

Don't take rejection personally

If you present an idea to your boss and he says, "I don't think it will work at this time," accept what he says at face value—it won't work at this time, but it may work later. Keep on trying. Most successful people seldom get their ideas accepted on the very first try.

Avoid mind reading

Jumping to conclusions results in negative thinking. For one thing, it never allows you to evaluate a situation and correct or change it. For example, when Marge discussed her raise with her boss, he was rather quiet and simply said, "I'm sorry, Marge, but I just can't come up with a raise for you at this time."

Marge decided that the reason she didn't get a raise was that she had refused to go out and pick up a present for her boss for his wife's birthday the week before.

By jumping to conclusions, Marge shortchanged herself. Had she discussed the matter with her boss and found out his real reasoning, she could have asked him when it might be appropriate for her to get another review. As a result, he may have agreed to re-evaluate her in six months instead of waiting the usual year.

Conclusion

A positive mental attitude can help make your dreams come true. By planning for your future and believing in your ability to be successful, you can accomplish whatever you put your mind to. Just like on a trip across the country, you're probably going to run into a few roadblocks along the way, but if you keep your mind focused on your ultimate goal, you will get there.

Chapter 4

Reversing a Negative Attitude

Even the most positive people can sometimes develop a negative attitude. The death of a loved one, financial setbacks, or health problems can all result in negative thinking.

Following are some tips for turning a negative attitude into a positive one.

Take time out

When your attitude begins to wane, spend a few minutes alone, talk to a friend, or take a short nap—anything that will help give you a break.

Examine what is making you feel bad

For example, you may feel the reason your attitude is so negative is that you've lost your job. If you really examine the situation carefully, however, you may discover that the real reason is that you feel incompetent because you were fired. In this situation, getting a new job will not necessarily help your negative attitude.

Develop a plan

Take the necessary steps to change things. If you've lost your confidence because you've lost your job, perhaps you can take a class that will help reassure you of your ability.

Focus on existing positives

If you lose your job, look at all the other things you have going for you: a good marriage, supportive family, understanding friends, etc.

Look to the future

Concentrate on how good you will feel after you have made changes. Focusing on positive events in the future will help get you through a difficult time.

When you're in a rut

If you don't take steps to get out of a rut, you may remain in it for much longer than necessary. If you remain in a rut too long, you will soon accept it as normal.

Here are some typical reasons people feel they are in a rut at work.

- They've become bored with their work.
- They feel like they want to try something different.
- They're in a dead-end position.

- Their take-home salary doesn't cover their expenses.
- They don't have a college degree or technical training.

For many people, staying in a rut is more comfortable than getting out of it. Getting out of a rut requires change, and many people fear change.

Here are some of the negatives associated with being stuck in a rut.

- Loss of energy and enthusiasm.
- Feeling as if you've lost control.
- Negative thinking.
- Loss of ambition.

If you feel as if you are stuck in a rut, the following tips may help you to climb out of it.

Isolate the problem

What is making you feel as if you are in a rut? If it's your home life, figure out exactly what the problem is. Are you frustrated because you feel like you never have enough time? Are you bored with your surroundings? Do you feel as if you never do anything for yourself? Is your relationship with your spouse a problem?

If it's work, figure out what there is about work that is getting you down. Are you bored? Is your boss difficult to work with? Are you spending too much time at the office?

Examine your options and seek solutions

Once you know what the problem is, you can figure out what options you have to correct it. If you don't have enough time to get things done at home, maybe you can enlist more of your spouse's help or hire people to do household chores. If you're bored with your job, see if there are opportunities to take on additional responsibilities or explore ways you can train for a promotion.

Keep things in perspective

For example, you may wrongly convince yourself that a job for minimum wage is all you're worth, so you resign yourself to the job you have. Just because you don't have a college education doesn't mean you can't return to school for training and get a better job.

Be flexible

There is more than one answer to a problem. Explore all your options.

Introduce variety

See if there is a way to change your job to make it more enjoyable or seek out additional responsibilities. For example, if you are a secretary in the communications department, maybe you can offer to gather news for the company newsletter. It also would give you an opportunity to learn new skills and add diversity to your job.

Consider a change

Look at other possible jobs both inside and outside your company.

Expand your circle of co-workers

Go to lunch with other co-workers or perhaps someone from a nearby office. New people will help give you a new perspective.

Look into professional organizations

This will give you a network of people outside your office with whom you can associate. Use them as sounding boards.

Change your appearance

If you are still wearing the same outfits you wore when you started your job five years ago, now is the time to start introducing new ones into your closet. Consider getting a new haircut, different makeup, or contact lenses. Also, try exercising regularly.

Introduce outside activities into your schedule

Take up a hobby, learn to play tennis, or join a health club.

Look to the future

For example, if you and your spouse are having problems, the main thing you should be concerned with is how to improve your relationship, not rehashing past problems. If you don't like your chosen career, decide what you would like to do.

Look up

It's been said that 80 percent of the people don't care about your problems and the other 20 percent are glad you have them! If you are depressed, the statement above will help you put life in perspective. But for a quick turnaround, jump-start your attitude by:

- Starting the day with good thoughts: "It's going to be a beautiful day."
- Greeting everyone you meet cheerfully, saying something positive.
- Responding, "I'm great," when people ask how you are.
- Spreading some good news around.
- Smiling—it adds value to your face.

Think about some things that always make you smile and list them below.

1. _____
2. _____
3. _____
4. _____
5. _____

Keep this list handy to pick you up and turn you around. Add at least one reason to smile each week.

Call on your friends

Spend more time with your family and friends. They can be a source of comfort and encouragement.

Conclusion

There is no reason to let a negative attitude drag you down. If you find yourself being particularly negative, take positive steps to turn your attitude around.

The only way to get out of a rut is to make changes in your life. Unfortunately, many people are afraid of change and therefore stay stuck in the same rut for years.

If you are in a rut, you have to choose between making a change that includes the risk of feeling uncomfortable and staying in a situation that makes you unhappy.

Chapter 5

Others and Your Attitude

Your attitude tells people what you will be like to work with. If you approach people with a smile and a cheerful greeting, they will perceive you as a happy person who is easy to get along with. If you are frowning or sullen, they will assume you are difficult to get along with.

Co-workers

If you don't develop positive personal relationships with your co-workers from the start, you may find it hard to do your job. No matter how talented you are, if you can't work with other people you probably won't get very far in your career.

This is particularly true when you are asked to work as part of a team. Build strong ties with co-workers. This doesn't mean you have to become good friends with everyone you work with, but it is important to get to know as much as you can about them. Knowing a little about co-workers' personal lives can help you relate to them better. For example, if you know that Becky has a sick child at home, you will be more understanding of her quiet moods.

Avoid comparing yourself with co-workers. Even if you have exactly the same job as another individual, you bring your own unique talents and abilities to your position.

My ideal co-worker

List below what you like about your "ideal" co-worker.

- _____
- _____
- _____
- _____
- _____

Now check the characteristics that also describe you.

Determine how you can develop the other skills or attitudes you listed for your ideal co-worker.

- _____
- _____
- _____
- _____
- _____

Through this process you will become the ideal co-worker to others. You also will improve your perception of yourself, raising your self-esteem.

Dealing with nonteam players

Sometimes you will be assigned to work on a project with an individual who isn't a team player. Here are some tips for getting this type of person to cooperate.

Be complimentary

Tell the individual how happy you are to be working with him and how important his expertise is to the project. By complimenting him on his ability, you will boost his self-confidence.

Tell him what you can contribute to the project

He may doubt your ability to do your part on the project. If you've worked on a similar project with another company, tell him about how you contributed to the project and the outcome of your efforts.

Suggest discussing the project over lunch

Getting away from the office will give you an opportunity to discuss the project in a nonthreatening environment.

Maintain a positive attitude

Hopefully your attitude will rub off on him. Don't let him drag you down. Focus on your goal.

Co-workers as sounding boards

A confidant at the office can help you put things in perspective and turn your attitude around.

For weeks Laura had been hoping her boss would give her a chance to work on a new assignment. Instead, he gave it to Bill, a new, less experienced employee.

Laura sat down with her friend Barb and said, "I can't understand it. I thought I was doing such a good job."

"Is that what you really think?" Barb asked. "Maybe he thought by giving the project to Bill it would take a little pressure off you."

Laura was putting so much stock in her initial hypothesis that she didn't take the time to explore the other possibilities.

Customers and your attitude

If you work with the public, a positive mental attitude is essential for success.

Think of the doctors you have been to. Although all probably have been highly qualified and skilled, chances are the ones you felt most confident and comfortable with were the ones with the positive, upbeat personalities.

The same is true in any customer-service job. In dealing with customers, put yourself in their shoes. Whom are you more likely to respond to: a salesperson with a smile who says, "May I help you?" or one who greets you with a frown?

If you are in a high-contact, customer-service position you may want to take a serious look at your job if you notice the following symptoms:

- Apathy.
- Withdrawal.

- Fatigue.
- Indifference.
- Irritability.
- Hostility.

If you experience these symptoms on a regular basis, you may suffer from what some psychologists term contact-overload syndrome. According to this theory, while some people have little or no problem dealing with customers on a daily basis, others find the experience uncomfortable and emotionally draining.

Recognizing you have difficulty dealing with customers is the first step in alleviating the problem. Here are some other suggestions:

Take breaks

Getting away from customers, even for five minutes, can be refreshing.

Stay in control

If a customer becomes angry with you, concentrate your efforts on finding a solution to the problem and avoid reacting to his anger.

Ask for help

If you find yourself in a situation where you feel you're losing control, ask your supervisor or a co-worker to take over for you.

Customer attitude

How do you like to be treated when you are shopping? List the behaviors or attitudes below.

+ Δ _____

+ Δ _____

+ Δ _____

+ Δ _____

+ Δ _____

+ Δ _____

+ Δ _____

+ Δ _____

+ Δ _____

Circle the plus (+) sign if you usually exhibit these behaviors or attitudes when working with your customers.

Circle the delta sign (Δ) if there's an opportunity for you to change a behavior or attitude to be more successful with your customers.

Record your top (+) strength: _____

Record your greatest opportunity (Δ) to improve: _____

Notes: _____

Take classes

Customer service classes can give you solid tips on dealing with difficult customers.

If none of these suggestions helps, you may be more comfortable in a job that doesn't require as much customer contact.

Your attitude and your boss

If you and your boss get along well, you probably have a positive attitude about your job and your chances for advancing in the company.

Like it or not, your boss has a certain amount of power over you. You may even feel he has control over whether you enjoy your work or not.

Granted, your boss can greatly influence how you feel about your job, but you have ultimate control.

If you dislike your boss or have negative feelings about him, find out why. Is it because he is younger than you? Does he lack confidence in you? Do you doubt his ability? Here are some tips:

Get to know your boss

One way to do this is to look carefully at his office. What kinds of things does he display? Knowing a little about his personality will help you to initiate conversations about things that interest him.

Follow your boss's cue

If he talks about his family, then you should feel free to talk about yours.

Accept your boss for the person he is

All bosses have different ways of managing. Try to look beyond management style issues and focus on positives. For instance, perhaps your boss isn't warm and outgoing but is consistently fair in the way he makes decisions.

Try to develop a compatible style

Work with him, not against him. If he is a morning person who likes to dictate his correspondence first thing in the day, get to work a little early. Don't make him have to chase you down.

If your boss has been rejecting your ideas lately, find out why and then take positive steps to change. Consider these possibilities:

Is your timing off?

When does he seem to be most productive, morning or afternoon? That's the time to present him with an idea.

Have you done your homework?

Is your proposal well-thought out and comprehensive?

Are you making yourself clear?

If you've left out any of the details, your boss simply may be confused about the value of what you're proposing.

How are your presentation skills?

Before presenting your idea, practice selling it to your boss in your mind. Be sure to anticipate and address concerns he may have regarding your idea.

If you still can't figure out why your boss is rejecting your ideas, ask him. If it is because you haven't done your homework, you can go back and present the idea again once you have all the details.

Optimism is contagious

If you exude a positive attitude about your job, chances are your co-workers will pick up on it and they too will become more positive.

If there is someone in your office who is always negative, make an extra effort to be positive and upbeat around him. If you share your positive attitude with your co-workers, they will be more cooperative and more willing to work with you the next time you need help.

Beware of negative people

On the job it's sometimes easy to get caught up in the frustrations and aggravations of co-workers. For example, if you find yourself going to lunch with people whose main topic of discussion is how bad things are at the office, you are probably going to return from lunch feeling down and negative.

Take the example of Steve. As a result of his boss's negative attitude, Steve sometimes has a hard time getting excited about his job. He enjoys what he does and has

How do you react?

Circle the answer that best reflects your response to the situation.

1. A co-worker has received a raise. You:

    A. Think you deserve a raise more than he.

    B. Feel happy for him.

    C. Neither of the above.

2. Your boss calls you into the office. You:

    A. Wonder what you did wrong.

    B. Feel ready for any problems he may have.

    C. Neither of the above.

3. A customer says you sold him the wrong product. You:

    A. Tell him he's wrong.

    B. Apologize and correct the situation.

    C. Neither of the above.

4. A customer takes up too much of your time. You:

    A. Get rid of him as soon as possible.

    B. Spend the time with the idea that it's good PR.

    C. Neither of the above.

5. You have a new idea to present to your supervisor. You:

    A. Are prepared and know that you can sell him the idea.

    B. Are worried and feel he probably won't like the idea.

    C. Neither of the above.

6. Your co-worker arrives at work every day with problems. You:
   A. Get rid of him knowing you can't solve his problems; you have enough of your own.
   B. Can't solve his problems, but tell him you have confidence in his ability to solve them.
   C. Neither of the above.

7. A client with a past-due account says he is mailing you a check today. You:
   A. Think, "I'll bet."
   B. Get ready to pay bills, because you'll have money tomorrow.
   C. Neither of the above.

8. Your boss calls you into the office and says he must let you go because of cutbacks. You:
   A. Wonder what you're going to do and think you didn't like working here anyway.
   B. Feel sad about losing contact with co-workers, but you've been wanting to make a change and are ready for some thing new.
   C. Neither of the above.

9. A customer comes in and wants to purchase an out-of-stock item. You:
   A. Tell him you're out of the item.
   B. Tell him you're temporarily out of the item but would be happy to check with other stores.
   C. Neither of the above.

Review your circled answers. Do you see a tendency to be positive and helpful or negative and self-defeating? These tendencies can be symptoms not only of a positive or negative outlook but of your level of self-esteem. Remember, how you react or project your feelings determines how others interact with you.

aspirations of moving up the corporate ladder, but every time he thinks he has a chance, his boss discourages him.

If Steve hopes to get ahead in the company, he is going to have to focus on what he wants. If there is a particular area of the company that interests him, he may even need to take steps to transfer to another department.

Improving your attitude toward others

Even if a co-worker displays negative traits, you can still work to make dealing with him pleasant. These tips may help you to be more successful.

Be understanding

Accept the fact that while you may be having a good day, the other person may not be. If he snaps at you, take it in stride.

Feel good about yourself

If you don't feel good about yourself, others won't either.

Display a sense of cooperation

When customers or co-workers feel that you sincerely want to help them, they are more likely to be cooperative.

Accept others for what they are

Don't expect a co-worker to complete a project in the same way that you would.

Let your enthusiasm show

Use gestures and move your body. Speak more clearly and quickly. Make eye contact. All these signals are cues to others that you are personally excited about what you are saying.

Try this "enthusiasm" exercise

If you do not perceive yourself as an expressive person, begin to practice expressiveness by talking to a favorite friend about what most excites you in life. Pay attention to your verbal as well as nonverbal behavior. Have someone videorecord your conversation so you can watch yourself later. You'll likely discover that when you talk about things that excite you, you do many of the things just described.

Conclusion

On the job, you may often be asked to complete a project as part of a team. Exhibit a spirit of cooperation with the people you have to work with and they invariably will cooperate with you. If a fellow worker proves to be less than cooperative, try to gain his cooperation.

Use friends and co-workers to help you maintain a positive outlook. They can be good sounding boards.

If you feel negatively about your boss, it will be to your advantage to try to change your feelings.

If you are in a customer-oriented job, a positive mental attitude is essential. In dealing with customers, the best thing to do is ask yourself how you would like to be treated. Then extend the same courtesy and helpfulness you would like to receive.

Chapter 6

Change and Your Attitude

Because change provokes fear, it can affect your attitude and the way you feel about your job. But it doesn't have to cause negative feelings. If handled correctly, change can be a positive rather than a negative.

Change that involves you

People who are unhappy with their jobs but choose to stay in the situation usually do so because they prefer the misery of the familiar to the uncertainty of change. Here are some typical fears people have about changing jobs.

What if I fail?

It's not likely. After all, you wouldn't have been hired if your new employer didn't believe you could handle the job.

What if I take the new job or position and then discover I really don't like it?

Don't look at it as an all-or-nothing proposition. If you don't like your new job, you can look for another one you do like.

What if the new job is worse than the job I have?

Plan on giving the new situation six months before you make any judgments and then examine the job objectively.

What if I can't get along with my new boss or co-workers?

Again, it's important to give any new situation time. You will need to adjust to new procedures, styles and personalities.

Change that involves the company

Corporate changes are frightening because they threaten not only your daily routine but also your livelihood. You may fear that you will lose your salary now or in the future.

Don't let change manage you; you manage change. This requires a calm, objective attitude—not one ruled by fear. Practice these strategies:

Unravel the truth

Make every attempt to find out the truth. Go to your boss and tell her about the rumors you've heard and ask her if they are true. (Keep in mind that she may not be able to discuss confidential information or that she may not know what is actually happening.)

Examine your options

If your boss confirms your fears, ask her what options are available to you. Are there other departments you can transfer to? Is the company planning to help you find a new job? Will the company offer severance pay and, if so, how much?

Be prepared

Put your resume in order and begin to "put out feelers." Finding out what other jobs are available will help you feel in control of the situation.

Be flexible

If your company is restructuring, chances are you will be asked to do things that are not routinely part of your job. Think of these tasks as ways to expand your resume.

Don't let change throw you

If you're being asked to do things that are unfamiliar or that require new skills, ask for help or take the initiative and find out about training.

Fear and your attitude

People generally see change as a threat that can affect them economically, psychologically, or socially. If you understand these perceived threats, you will be better able to deal with them.

Economic threat

Instead of exerting all your energy worrying about losing money, concentrate on ways to improve your financial situation. This may mean getting a job outside the company or setting your sights on a higher-paying job within your company.

Psychological threat

What will the change mean to you? Will you have to learn something new? Will your position or authority be affected? All can influence your psychological well-being.

Let's think about it

Analyze each threat carefully. If you have to learn a new skill, think of it as a way to expand your experience.

Circle the answer that best describes how you would deal with these situations.

1. You don't like your job but you've been there five years. Will you:
   A. Stay, waiting for retirement?
   B. Stay, but send out some resumes?
   C. Leave and know you'll find something else?

2. You like your employer but the job's not rewarding or challenging. Will you:
   A. Talk to your supervisor about changing positions?
   B. Look for projects you can volunteer to do?
   C. Leave the company?

3. You are an accountant but feel this is not what you want to do for the rest of your life. Will you:

   A. Stay because you're good at it and make a good income?

   B. Talk to a career counselor about a new career?

   C. Quit and do something else while considering a new career?

4. Every day you work, go home, watch TV, sleep, and go back to work with "catch up" work on the weekend. You realize you're in a rut. You:

   A. Keep it up because it may not be exciting but it's predictable.

   B. Take tennis lessons after work or maybe even a cooking class.

   C. Quit your job and move

5. You have reached the age of 40 and realize there are a lot of things you wanted to do but haven't. You:

   A. Like the way things are, and these things aren't important to you anymore.

   B. Pick out the most important and decide how to do them

   C. Quit your job and take some college courses

If you circled the first (A) answer, you may be avoiding change. If you circled the second (B) answer you may be overly cautious with changes, and if you circled the last (C) answer you like to make change happen.

The tips in this chapter will help you deal with change. Remember, your success or failure to meet the challenges of change depends on your mental attitude.

Social threat

A new job, whether it's within your company or with a new company, means that you probably will be working with a new boss and new co-workers.

Think of a new job as a way to meet new people. Handle the situation the same way you would a party where you didn't know all the guests. Don't wait for someone to ask you to join her for lunch. Approach her and ask if you can join her.

Tips on accepting change

Confronting change can broaden your career horizons and build your self-confidence. Here are some tips to help you accept change.

Take it at face value

Realize that change is a part of all companies. If a company doesn't change, it will become stagnant and soon fail to be a contender in the marketplace.

Seek out the benefit to you

Some benefits may include new skills or responsibilities, meeting new people who can help your career, or building strong relationships with your boss and co-workers.

Keep an open mind

Maintaining a positive attitude and an open mind can be the most important way you support your boss during a period of change. This step alone can contribute to your job security.

Be patient

All changes have an adjustment period. For example, when Jane decided to change teaching jobs, she was excited. But throughout the first semester, Jane found herself increasingly unhappy. The principal expected her to do things she didn't have to do at her old school, and the teachers all seemed to have different methods of teaching.

Jane didn't give herself enough of an adjustment period. By the second semester, however, Jane began to fall into the routine and felt more at ease with her new school.

Visualize the change

What will your work area look like? Visualize yourself walking into your new job and feeling confident and self-assured.

Develop a support system

Recruit the support of your family and friends. They can act as good resources and provide you with the positive reinforcement you need.

How change affects your attitude

Typically, there are four phases involved in every change.

1. *Denial.* You continue to think about the past and concentrate on how much you enjoy your job. Denial creates a negative attitude because it prevents you from taking the necessary steps to move forward.

2. *Resistance.* During the resistance phase you may experience depression, anger, frustration, and fear. It can be healthy to share these emotions with your family and co-workers. Be careful, however, not to allow these conversations to turn into complaint sessions; look for positive solutions.

3. *Exploration.* Explore ways to make the situation more positive. This may come in the form of putting your resume together or looking at ways to get additional training.

4. *Commitment.* Put the past behind you and begin to concentrate your efforts on the future.

Conclusion

You may find yourself faced with a technological change, a change in position, change in boss, change in workload, or change in companies. If you don't look at change in a positive way, your morale will suffer.

Changes are a natural part of any company (and life as well). The more flexible and adaptable you are, the easier the change will be on you and the more likely you will stay with the company.

Chapter 7

Attitudes and Success

If you are self-assured and confident, you will have a positive attitude and believe you can accomplish anything. Fear of success, fear of failure, and inferiority complexes can all affect the way you feel about yourself and thus influence your ability to succeed.

Fear of success

Have you ever decided to do something that would result in a major improvement in your life, but then never followed through? If so, you may have experienced the fear of success. People fear success for various reasons:

Fear of negative consequences

Nancy has been up for the same promotion three times. Every time, she does something that makes her boss reconsider.

Nancy really wants the promotion, but if she gets it, she will be making more money than her husband for the first time. Nancy fears he will somehow feel threatened and find her less appealing.

Fear of ultimately failing

Some people are afraid that if they succeed they may ultimately fail. Jill wants to move into the secretarial pool but deep down inside she is afraid that if she gets the job, she may not be able to do it. Therefore, she continually sabotages her chances of getting it.

Fear of being stuck

Jeff likes working with computers and is good at it. His boss wants to promote him to the computer department, but every time the boss gets ready to do so, Jeff makes a major error. He is afraid that if his boss moves him to the computer department, he won't like it and he will be stuck there forever.

Fear of outdoing their parents

When Mike graduated from high school, his father got him a job at the plant where he works.

Mike's boss recognizes that he has talent in marketing. The boss wants to give him a management position in the marketing department. Mike really wants it, but when the marketing manager interviewed him for the job, Mike came across as extremely negative and uninterested.

Deep down, Mike is afraid of climbing higher in the company than his father.

Overcoming the fear of success

Here are some situations that may help you realize you are sabotaging your efforts.

- Do you find yourself at certain key times repeating mistakes you usually don't make otherwise?
- Have you lost enthusiasm for your work?
- Have you noticed a change in your personality?

Take the necessary steps to overcome your fear. The following tips may help.

Analyze your fear

Figure out what you are really afraid of. Jill is not afraid of failing the initial test; she is afraid of failing once she gets the job.

Attack the fear head-on

Nancy fears that her husband will feel threatened if she makes more money than he does. The only way for her to find out is to discuss the matter openly and honestly with him.

Decide on the worst possible scenario

Ask yourself, "What is the worst that could happen?" Take Jeff, who fears moving into the computer department. The worst thing that could happen is he would have to go back to his old job or find a new one.

Dealing with failure

Failure can have a devastating effect on your life, but it also can be turned into a positive experience. Think of failure as an education. If you don't recognize your mistakes, you will never learn from them.

Failure is one way for us to perfect our plans in life. For example, let's say you are on a weight-loss program. Success spurs you on, and over the next two months you lose an average of two pounds a week. But then something happens. You gain a pound.

This minor setback is an important key to helping you perfect your weight-loss program. If you begin to watch your calorie intake more carefully and resume your exercise program, you will once again begin losing weight.

Failure and risks

Risk, failure, and change are all key steps in personal and career advancement. If you don't take risks, you will never get ahead.

Sally worked for a small distributorship. When the job of office manager became available, she discussed the job with her boss and was pleased when she got it.

Sally was good at every aspect of her job except one: she was afraid to take risks because she feared failure. What the boss wanted was someone who would take charge and make decisions—even wrong ones—occasionally.

All of us fail at one time or another. The following tips will help take the sting out of the experience.

Take responsibility

When you've done something wrong, admit it immediately and tell your boss what you intend to do to make amends.

Analyze the failure

Take the time to figure out why you failed. Learn from your mistakes.

Don't dwell on failure

Move on! If you dwell on failure, it will paralyze you.

Keep things in perspective

Just because you failed at one thing does not mean your entire life is a failure.

Turn to loved ones

When you suffer a severe failure, such as being fired from your job, your loved ones can provide you with moral support. Discuss how you feel and get your fears, anger, and frustrations off your chest.

Accept failure for what it is

Failure is a temporary setback. Avoid thinking of it as a life-or-death situation.

Give it time

Give yourself sufficient time to recover from the experience, but don't let it drag on too long.

Avoid negative self-talk

Sometimes when you fail at one thing you may begin to doubt your ability in other areas. For example, Sue told her boss she made plane reservations for him for 7 p.m. Actually, the plane left at 7 a.m. and her boss missed his flight. "I'm incompetent," Sue told herself. But she is not incompetent. She made a simple mistake. And there is a positive side...Sue has learned to always check and double-check reservations.

Consider training

If your failure is a result of a lack of technical expertise, seek out training. It will help make you feel more confident.

Failure in another's eyes

Sometimes we may feel confident of the job we're doing but a co-worker or boss may make us feel like a failure. Mark's new boss, Linda, knew that her employees liked their former boss, who had retired, and feared they would not give her a chance.

Instead of explaining her concerns to her employees and asking for their cooperation, Linda often criticized their work. Mark, who felt like a success when he worked for his former boss, suddenly began to feel like a failure.

Don't let another person undermine your confidence. Take the following steps:

Talk it out

If the problem is your boss, ask him if he is dissatisfied with your work. If he is feeling threatened, this may make him see that you want to work with him, not against him.

Assure your boss of your loyalty

Tell him how much you enjoy working with him and how much you have learned from him. These kinds of statements will help to assure him you are on his team.

Make your boss look good

If you can do something to make your boss look good to *his* boss, you are bound to win him over.

Remain positive

Don't let a negative attitude show through. If your boss doubts your ability, a negative attitude will only confirm his fears.

Rebuilding your image when you fail

Because of an error you made, your company has lost a major client. Following are some tips to help you rebuild a positive attitude toward yourself and your job.

Avoid paranoia

Don't assume that just because you made one mistake everyone is waiting for you to make another one.

Be positive and optimistic

When talking about aspirations, don't use words such as "try," "attempt," or "may." Instead use words such as "will," "can," and "are." There is no room for tentativeness and qualifiers in statements of vision. Sure, there are reasons why something might not happen. There may also be many contingencies. But this does not mean you have to be excessively Pollyannaish or unrealistic. Go ahead and think and talk about the hardships and difficult conditions. But don't dwell on them. Recognize that great achievements require hard work.

Analyze the situation

How bad is the situation? Have major players in the company really lost their confidence in you?

What does it all mean?

Does it mean that you will be uncomfortable around your co-workers until the whole thing blows over or does it mean that you won't be able to get your job done? Be realistic.

Change your behavior

Prove that you have learned from your mistake and you can do the job.

Be patient

Don't expect to rebuild your reputation overnight. In the meantime, spend your time concentrating on positives.

Tips for avoiding failure

Here are some tips to help you avoid failure.

1. *Have a backup plan.* Whenever you have responsibility for a major project, always have a backup plan in place. Take the example of Jerri. Her boss asked her to plan the annual company party. Jerri decided to do something different and planned a picnic. But on the day of the picnic, it rained. Few people showed up, and those who did complained about how poorly the event was planned.

   If Jerri had had an alternate plan, she could have avoided this failure. For example, she could have designated a rain day or established an alternate location inside.

2. *Don't bite off more than you can chew.* Let's say your boss tells you he is looking for someone to develop a company newsletter. Unfortunately, because you have no experience, you spend weeks spinning your wheels but never get an issue out. A more prudent approach would have been to help your boss find someone who could act as editor and then offer to help that person.

3. *Get training when you need it.* If your boss asks you to do something and you don't have the expertise, admit it openly and tell him you would like to receive training.

Fear

Do you control and use fear to motivate and drive your will to succeed, or is fear a defeating element in your life? List below situations in your career when you experienced fear.

+ — _____

+ — _____

+ — _____

+ — _____

+ — _____

Circle (-) if you perceived the fear as a negative motivator, (+) if you perceived the fear as a positive motivator. Did you recognize the fear at the time? If you could replay time, how would you:

•Change the negative, fearful situation into a positive one?

•Use fear to your advantage?

•Use fear to give you energy for the task ahead?

Remember, "Don't be afraid to take a big step if one is indicated. You can't cross a chasm in two small jumps."
—David Lloyd George

Feelings of inferiority

People with inferiority complexes are afraid they can't keep up and that someone will realize they are incompetent.

Many people with inferiority complexes practice negative self-talk. Take Doug, for example, who was hired by a major advertising firm. Although he was hired for being the most qualified applicant, he told his family and friends, "There must not have been many qualified applicants for this job."

If you find yourself making negative statements, stop and turn them around into positive ones.

Impostor complex

Some authorities estimate that as many as 70 percent of all successful people feel like impostors at one time or another. Although most learn how to deal with the situation, others let it cripple them and keep them from succeeding.

Following are some typical symptoms of people who suffer from the impostor complex.

- They avoid taking promotions.
- They feel guilty when they succeed.
- They spend time focusing on what they haven't achieved rather than what they have achieved.
- They attribute their success to luck.
- They are embarrassed when someone congratulates them.

A New Attitude

People who believe they are impostors feel that way for a variety of reasons:

- They had overly critical parents or parents who praised them too much.

- They climbed the corporate ladder faster than normal.

- They found themselves making more money than they ever thought possible and at a young age.

- They are a "first" in their company, such as the first woman or minority or the youngest person ever to hold an executive position with the company.

If you suffer from the impostor syndrome, you can learn to accept your successes in life. Here are some tips:

- Realize that the inability to take credit for your own success is a problem that may prevent you from succeeding in the future.

- Think back on the messages your parents gave you as a child. Were they negative? If they were always positive, did you feel you deserved the praise?

- Accept that it is okay not to be perfect all the time.

- Accept that it is okay not to know everything.

Success chart

Success is a habit you can make happen. Once it happens, you can make it happen again and again. Choices in your personal life affect your successes as much as challenges or problems.

Begin this chart the date you graduated. Next, record the year you made key personal choices (marriage, children, major purchases, etc.). Next, do the same for career successes (promotions, awards, career changes), followed by career challenges (termination, financial crisis, layoff, etc.).

Year	Personal Choices	Career Successes	Career Challenges

Do you notice any trends? Perhaps a challenge was followed by increased activity or inactivity. Did one success follow another? Spend time reflecting on what you've recorded and update your chart periodically.

Conclusion

All of us suffer failure at one time or another. You can turn failure into a positive experience and learn from your mistakes.

A New Attitude

Any time you take a risk, there is a chance for failure. But if you're not willing to take risks, you won't move forward.

Take the right attitude for failure and you can make it work for you. Think of failure as a beginning, not an end.

Chapter 8

Physical Appearance and Health

If you look good and feel good, you will see yourself in a positive light and project that same image to others.

Making the most of what you have

The way you feel about your overall physical appearance affects the way you appear to others. For example, if you are overweight, you may wear oversized clothes or slouch when you sit or stand, hoping to blend into the background. Both behaviors send a negative message to your co-workers and boss.

To feel good about yourself, you need to identify your positive physical attributes and focus on them. Although you cannot totally ignore the negatives, there is no reason to dwell on them.

If a permanent solution exists to help you change the negative into a positive, take advantage of it. If not, find a way to make the best of the situation.

Sometimes we encounter temporary negative feelings about our looks. A bad permanent, a few extra pounds, or even a broken arm can make us feel unattractive and cause a loss of confidence.

At times like these, it is also important to maintain a sense of humor. Think of how you will feel about the situation in six months.

The way you dress

Clothes may not really make the man or woman, but they do have a great deal to say about how you feel about yourself.

- Are you still wearing the same outfits you wore five years ago?
- If you've gotten a promotion, have you updated your clothes to go along with the new job?
- Are your shoes polished and your clothes clean and well-pressed?

Knowing that you have up-to-date styles that complement your figure will help you feel good about the way you're dressed.

If you've recently gotten a promotion to management, look at what others in similar positions are wearing. You don't have to become a clone of someone else, but observing others will help you define the image you are looking for.

Your physical appearance

List below the physical attributes (including wardrobe) you want to change about yourself. On the right, list three actions you can take to improve that particular physical attribute.

Physical Attributes to Change	Actions to Take for Improvement
1.	1.
	2.
	3.
2.	1.
	2.
	3.
3.	1.
	2.
	3.
4.	1.
	2.
	3.
5.	1.
	2.
	3.

List below the positive aspects of your physical appearance.

1. _____
2. _____
3. _____
4. _____
5. _____

Well-polished shoes and neatly pressed clothes tell other people you care about details. One executive says he will not hire an applicant with unpolished shoes because he believes that poor grooming reflects directly on the kind of work the applicant will do.

Health and your attitude

The way you feel about yourself impacts your health as it does your physical appearance. To evaluate yourself, answer these questions:

Are you getting enough sleep?	Yes	No
Are you drastically overweight or underweight?	Yes	No
Is your diet well-balanced?	Yes	No
Do you have high cholesterol or high blood pressure?	Yes	No
Do you exercise regularly?	Yes	No

If you experience chronic physical problems, make an appointment with your doctor. Getting a checkup may be just what you need to get your body and your attitude in shape.

If you are overweight, begin a sensible diet and exercise program. Your doctor can steer you in the right direction.

If you're not getting enough sleep, figure out why and find a way to incorporate more time for rest into each day.

Your health checkup

Rate each of your following health attributes by placing the appropriate letter in the status column: I for Ideal or NI for Needs Improvement.

Attribute	Status
Weight	_____
Diet	_____
Blood pressure	_____
Cholesterol level	_____
Exercise	_____
Posture	_____
Sleep habits	_____
Nervous habits/stress	_____

Circle the NIs and compare them with your information in the previous exercise. You may have a weight problem that you identified as an opportunity to change. However, you may not have realized that your poor sleep habits affect your ability to change your weight—in other words, you are too tired to exercise.

Let's look at another example. If you change your diet, it can affect your weight and cholesterol level. Exercise can impact all areas.

Start with the most critical factor that impacts multiple areas to get the greatest improvement.

Conclusion

Your physical appearance is just as important to your positive mental attitude as your confidence in your skills and ability.

Create your own style. Find styles and colors that look best on you and use them to create a positive look.

Don't forget to take care of your body. If you are in poor physical shape, you will have a difficult time being positive about anything in your life.

Chapter 9

Work Attitudes and Job Satisfaction

Adults spend much of their lives working. If you don't like what you do or the people you work with, you will soon find yourself dissatisfied and unhappy with your life in general.

What are the qualities of your ideal job? If you are like most people, you probably would list many of the following:

- Good pay.

- Nice office environment.

- Ability to make decisions.

- Cooperative, supportive boss.

- Good benefits.

- Challenging work and meaningful responsibilities.

Job satisfaction

Although job satisfaction is driven by some external factors, it also has to do in large part with your attitude. Even if your job isn't perfect, you can still develop a positive attitude about it. The key is to determine what factors provide you with job satisfaction and then concentrate on trying to achieve them.

Job satisfaction includes these key elements:

- **Reasonable pay**—You feel you are being paid a fair and reasonable wage for the job you do.

- **Potential for advancement**—You see opportunities to advance within your company.

- **Work environment**—Your work environment is pleasant and safe.

- **Status**—You are comfortable with your position within the company.

- **Boss**—You believe that he is supportive and fair.

- **Working conditions**—Your job offers enough variety to keep you from getting bored.

- **Job security and benefits**—You are not constantly afraid of losing your job, and the benefits you receive are adequate.

- **Career aspirations**—Your job is in line with your overall career goals.

- **Personal satisfaction**—You feel confident and good about the job you do.

The priority placed on these factors will vary from individual to individual. Following are some typical reasons workers give for being dissatisfied with their jobs.

- **Poor working environment**—You work around noisy or hazardous machinery, or you sit at a desk all day with little opportunity to move around.

- **Poor interpersonal relationships**—You don't get along with your boss or co-workers.

- **No freedom**—You are closely supervised and have no decision-making ability.

- **No challenge**—You have no opportunity to use your initiative or creativity.

- **Too much work**—You always have more work than you can possibly handle.

- **Dead end**—You have gone as far as you can go in the company.

- **Job security**—Your ability to keep your job is tied to factors you have no control over—the economy, politics, the whim of your supervisor, etc.

- **Job status**—You are low on the totem pole, and you are made to feel that way.

Creating job satisfaction

You may not have control over the working conditions or the pay, but you do have control over the way you view your situation.

Your ideal job

Take a few minutes and brainstorm by yourself or with an individual who knows you well. Identify all the characteristics you need in an "ideal job." (Be honest so you can accurately assess your job satisfaction.)

1. _____

2. _____

3. _____

4. _____

5. _____

6. _____

7. _____

8. _____

9. _____

10. _____

11. _____

12. _____

13. _____

14. _____

15. _____

Circle the characteristics that are in your current job. Place an X by the three characteristics that are most important to you. Are any of the three in your current job? Do they involve you or do they involve the company?

Here are some tips to help you turn the negatives about your job into positives.

Look for different ways to do your job

If you usually open the mail first, type correspondence second, and do your filing last, change the order in which you perform these tasks.

Learn more about your company

Do you know how your specific job impacts the company? Find out how what you do influences the final product. Talk to your boss, read company publications or get a copy of the annual report.

Learn more about the industry

Find out what the latest products are and where your company stands among the competitors.

Follow the company's stock

Predict what you think the company's stock will do each day and then check to see how you did.

Build a positive relationship

Choose a co-worker you haven't gotten along with or one you don't know very well and build a positive working relationship.

Join a professional organization

Find a professional organization in your field and join it. You will probably find that your colleagues have the same frustrations you do. Find out how they handle various situations.

Attend a seminar or take a class

Updating your skills will not only make you feel more proficient; it will boost your self-confidence if you decide to look for another job.

Job burnout

Learn to recognize the warning signals of burnout:

- You feel bored and restless.

- You dread going to work in the morning.

- You feel panicked.

- You're confused. You don't know what you want to do.

- You're working just as hard as you always have, if not harder, but you are getting less done.

- You've become cynical.

- You've become forgetful.

- You are suffering an increasing number of physical ailments.

- You're always tired.

Why people experience job burnout

People suffer from job burnout for various reasons:

- They attempt to do too much. Many women who tried to fit the mold of superwoman in the 80s burned out.
- They feel unappreciated. They're doing as much as you physically can, but their boss still wants more.
- Boredom. They've learned everything there is to learn about their job and it lacks challenge.

The effects of burnout

Burnout affects you physically, emotionally and mentally and can turn a positive attitude into a negative one. Let's look at each aspect:

- *Physical.* You are more fatigued than normal. You also may find you are more susceptible to illness.
- *Emotional.* You feel trapped and helpless. You may even begin to exhibit neurotic behaviors.
- *Mental.* You begin to look at things in more negative terms.

Treatment for burnout

The most important thing to do is regain control.

1. *Uncover the cause.* Figure out exactly what is causing you to feel burned out. For example, do you have extra work because a co-worker left? If so, ask your boss if some of your work can be distributed to other employees.

2. *Add balance to your life.* Take it one step at a time. For example, if you have been spending every Saturday at the office, gradually cut Saturdays out of your workweek altogether.

3. *Take care of yourself physically.* If you haven't had time for exercise, incorporate it into your schedule.

4. *Take time off.* Getting away from the situation completely will do wonders for your perspective. Take vacation time or, if necessary, a leave of absence.

5. *Speak up.* If you're unhappy with some aspect of your job, talk it over with your boss. It won't do you any good to suffer in silence.

6. *Talk it out.* Talk to your spouse or a friend about what you're feeling or, if the situation warrants it, seek professional counseling.

Workaholism

Workaholics have a distorted view of the importance of their jobs. Their work consumes them to the exclusion of everything and everyone else.

As a result, if they lose their jobs or fail at work, they feel they have lost everything. Often, because they have sacrificed their families, friends, and relationships for their jobs, there is no one to help them pick up the pieces.

People become workaholics for a variety of reasons:

- *They are tired of taking care of others.* This can sometimes be the case with a new mother. She becomes emotionally drained and, as a result, begins to spend more and more time at work to avoid spending time with her child.

- *They are trying to avoid dwelling on something negative that has happened in their lives.* Many times, after a divorce or the death of a loved one, a person will throw himself into his work to avoid thinking about an unhappy situation.

- *They are still living with a message they received as a child.* Some workaholics were praised and rewarded for good work as children. Thus, as adults, they work harder and harder to gain approval and acceptance.

The symptoms of workaholism

Here are a few of the warning signals of workaholism:

- You take time off or go on vacation and can't relax.

- You are depressed.

- You experience stress that takes a toll on you as well as your family.

- Your family takes on more and more of your responsibilities around the house.

- You spend less time with your children. They cry when you leave and won't let you alone when you are home.

- You've lost contact with friends.

Am I a workaholic

Take a moment to evaluate how you spend your time. Ask yourself, "When was the last time I..."

1. Read a book for enjoyment?
2. Attended a play or concert?
3. Invited friends over for the evening?
4. Played with my children?
5. Invited friends (not relatives) over for a meal?
6. Took a two-week vacation?
7. Exercised?
8. Enjoyed taking a drive?
9. Delegated a project at work?
10. Took a class or lesson for enjoyment?
11. Participated in a hobby?
12. Attended a social (personal) function?
13. Took a mental time-out day?
14. Talked with my significant other about his or her personal interests?
15. Sat down to eat three consecutive meals with my family?

Do you see a trend in this exercise that appears to focus only on your career? Everyone needs diversity in life. Some of the above activities may not interest you, but watch for the tell-tale signs of workaholic self-talk: "When I have time, I'd like to..." etc.

Continue by completing the following sentence: "When I have time, I'd like to..."

1. _____
2. _____
3. _____
4. _____
5. _____
6. _____
7. _____
8. _____
9. _____
10. _____

Put one of the above activities on your calendar to experience or accomplish in the next month. Each month review this list and put another activity on your calendar.

Watch for signs of workaholic self-talk.

Overcoming workaholism

Take a piece of paper and write down how many hours you think you currently work. Then, for the next week, log the actual amount of time you spend at the office, indicating the time spent on each task. You may be shocked by how much time you actually spend at work.

From your log, figure out why you are taking so long to do your work. Do you have more work than you can handle? Are you a perfectionist? Are you using outdated equipment? Are you trying to avoid problems at home?

Once you have figured out where the problem lies, you can take steps to correct it. You may even want to consider taking a time-management course. It will help you take control of the situation. If you still have a tendency to overwork, consider professional counseling.

Perfectionism

There is nothing wrong with trying to do things to the best of your ability, but when always doing your best becomes an obsession, it can cause you problems. Here are some of the traits of perfectionists:

- **You procrastinate.** You put off doing or completing tasks because you are afraid you won't do them perfectly.

- **You don't take risks.** You are afraid that if you try something new you won't be able to do it perfectly, so you don't even try.

- **You spend your time doing unimportant or menial tasks.** You spend hours cleaning off your desk each night or dusting your office. You waste time doing only those things you are certain to succeed at.

To overcome your perfectionistic tendencies, try the following:

- **Adjust your standards.** This doesn't mean to start doing shoddy work; it simply means you shouldn't be so hard on yourself.

- **Establish priorities.** Make sure you get your most important tasks done first and then handle the menial chores.

- **Establish time limits.** Some perfectionists spend an inordinate amount of time working to get something perfect. Assign yourself deadlines for even the smallest chores.

Conclusion

If you are happy and content with your job, chances are you will have a more positive outlook on life. If you develop negative habits, such as workaholism or perfectionism, your attitude will suffer.

Burnout, workaholism, and perfectionism all can affect the way you feel about your job. If you recognize any of these problems, take steps to correct them before your attitude, and ultimately your work, suffer.

Chapter 10

Stress

Although stress can be caused by major upheavals such as changing jobs or finding out that your company is involved in a hostile takeover, it also can be the result of a minor irritation such as broken office equipment or too many distractions. One research study shows that daily hassles are more likely to affect a person's moods and attitudes than the major misfortunes in life.

Stress can be caused by positive events as well as negative ones. You may experience just as much stress if you get a promotion as you do if you get fired.

If you look at stress in positive terms, it will motivate you to succeed. If you look at it negatively, it will prevent you from succeeding.

What makes you crazy?

List the things that drive you up the wall in the "I Get Crazy When" column below. Some examples could be clutter, tardiness and interruptions.

	I get crazy when:	**I can help by:**
1.	_____	_____
2.	_____	_____
3.	_____	_____
4.	_____	_____
5.	_____	_____
6.	_____	_____
7.	_____	_____
8.	_____	_____
9.	_____	_____
10.	_____	_____
11.	_____	_____
12.	_____	_____
13.	_____	_____
14.	_____	_____
15.	_____	_____

Next select your *top* "Crazy" and in the "I can help" column list the steps you will take to eliminate it. Continue each day to expand your plan to eliminate your crazy list.

You can't eliminate all the craziness, but if you significantly reduce the items on the list, you'll reduce your overall stress level and improve your productivity and attitude.

The effects of stress

Regardless of the source of the stress, if it is chronic and left untreated, it can affect you both physically and mentally. Physically, you may feel tired and irritable or suffer from headaches or neck aches. Mentally, you may begin to question your abilities or develop a negative attitude.

Research shows that people in the lower echelons of their companies are more susceptible to stress and its negative effects than those at the top. Employees on the lower rungs of the corporate ladder often have high-demand jobs and little control.

According to one study, laborers and secretaries are at the top of the list of workers whose jobs cause the most stress-related illnesses. Others in the top 10 include waiters and waitresses, farm owners, and office managers.

Whether stress is good or bad will determine how you handle the situation. If you are under stress because you have accepted a job that requires more expertise than you have, find a way to gain the skills you need. Don't simply tell yourself you can't do it.

Handling stress

If stress is having a negative effect on your attitude, here are some tips for regaining control.

Identify the stressor

Is it the fact that you have too much work, or do you feel you are in over your head?

Daily stressors

List the daily activities that often cause you stress and potential ways to alleviate them.

	Stressors:	Alleviate by:
1.	_____	_____
2.	_____	_____
3.	_____	_____
4.	_____	_____
5.	_____	_____

Alleviating the "small stressors" each day will enable you to be better prepared for the larger, unpredictable stressors.

Remember, it's the small things that make life worthwhile as well as "make you crazy." Add the little things you find important and worthwhile; eliminate the negative small things.

Determine if it really is a problem

For example, if your company is laying off workers, it is definitely a problem. However, a rumor that your company *may* lay off workers is not.

Decide if it is something you can control

If your company is going to lay off workers, you have the option of getting another job. If, on the other hand, your boss is not doing her work and you fear that her boss may question you about what your boss does, you have little control over the situation.

Take action

If you have control over the situation, look for ways to minimize the stress. For example, concentrate your efforts on finding another job.

If you find yourself reacting negatively, then change. Start small. The next time you are faced with a minor irritant, decide that you will not let it make you feel negative. Practice this process again and again until you are able to do it with more important issues.

Here are some tips that may help you cope with the negative effects of stress.

- Participate in physical activity.

- Talk to friends and family.

- Create a balance in your life with work, family, and recreation.

- Keep yourself in good health.

- Accept the things you can't change.

Conclusion

Don't let stress on the job or at home affect your work. If the stress in your life is chronic, find a way to handle it so it doesn't have a negative effect on your attitude. Remember to recognize those small daily stressors and alleviate them.

Chapter 11

Problems Outside of Work

Sometimes problems outside of work affect your attitude about your job. A serious illness, the death of a loved one, or marital problems all can affect the way you do your job and the way you feel about it.

Take the example of Betty. Betty's husband is out of town five days each week on business, which leaves raising the children during the week up to her. She has no one to share the responsibility with and feels she never has time for herself.

Lately, Betty finds she has been snapping at her co-workers and instructing her secretary to keep people out of her office. Without meaning to, Betty is letting her frustrations at home affect her life at the office.

A positive mental attitude is important to help you guard against letting this happen. If problems at home are creeping into your job, do two things:

1. *Make a conscious effort to separate work and home.* On the way to work, tell yourself you're leaving your personal problems at home. Visualize closing your door and leaving your problems locked inside. Do the same thing when you leave work.

2. *Determine how you can change your circumstances at home or at work to reduce the pressure.* For example, Betty has asked her children to give her 45 minutes of quiet time when she gets home in the evenings. She has done the same thing at the office, asking her subordinates not to disturb her for the first hour of the day so she can get her day organized.

Support contract

This "support contract" can be used to help reduce stress in your life. Use it to obtain agreement from significant others, such as family, to give you needed support. On the left side of the "contract" identify what you need help with, and on the right side have each support person record how he will help.

I need help with:	I will help by:
1. _____	_____
	(name)
2. _____	_____
	(name)
3. _____	_____
	(name)
_____	_____
Signature	Signature(s)

Encourage others to use this "contract." It has the potential to build a foundation for a powerful support network.

Life changes

When you encounter a major setback in your life such as divorce, losing a job, or a death in the family, it may be the time to get out your "When I have time, I'd like to..." list. These activities can give you a new direction or, at the least, give you some time to adjust. You might even find a new career. This could be a good time to look at the changes you've been wanting to make and give you that extra lift to get you going!

Start now by completing the following sentence:

When I have time, I'd like to...

1. _____

2. _____

3. _____

4. _____

5. _____

6. _____

7. _____

8. _____

9. _____

10. _____

Which of these do you feel are essential for you to pursue now?

Major problems

Sometimes something so negative happens that we have a hard time seeing anything positive. The death of a loved one, divorce, and major health problems can cause us to lose hope.

The best way to mend your attitude in these situations is to accept what has happened and find a way to get beyond the incident. Dwelling on how miserable you feel is not going to help. Looking ahead to the future will.

Here are some suggestions for getting on with your life.

Find something to occupy your time

Redirect your focus from how bad you feel to how good you can make someone else feel. Take the example of Marsha. After her husband walked out, a friend called and asked her to help with a major fund-raising project. Marsha agreed and before she knew it she was working practically every night on the project. Suddenly she noticed she was no longer distracted at work.

Take off your victim blinders

If you always focus your energy and attention on what is missing from your life, life itself may pass you by. By always wearing your blinders, it becomes easy to completely forget there is more to life than what you see yourself missing, You simply cannot see fun, laughter, love, productivity and adventure as a *choice*.

When you choose to be positive, positive things start to happen. What you focus on expands in your life. What you radiate, you attract.

List the positives in your life

Write down everything in your life that is positive. For example, if you are getting a divorce, positive things in your life may include having healthy children and enjoying your work.

Plan for the future

If you've just lost your job, concentrate on thinking about how much you will enjoy your new one. If you're going through a divorce, plan on taking a vacation to get away.

Engage in positive self-talk

Turn statements such as, "My life will never be the same" into "My life will be different, but I will work to make it better."

Talk to family and friends

Sometimes just talking with a friend or a family member about a bad situation can be therapeutic.

Give yourself time

Don't expect to get over the pain or shock immediately. Give yourself the time you need to heal.

Dealing with problems

Remember that no matter what the problem, there is someone who has a worse problem than you do.

When a crisis occurs in your life, take these steps to regain control.

Take a deep breath

Take a minute to step back and look at the problem realistically.

Work on finding a solution

After you've identified the problem, begin working on finding a solution. If possible, try to wait a little while before exploring options. If you can, "sleep on it" before making any firm decision on how you plan to handle it.

Consider all the options

For example, if you didn't get a raise, list the options you have available. Solutions may be to: (a) cut back on your expenses, (b) ask your boss for a smaller raise that will allow you to meet your expenses, (c) get a part-time job.

A visualization exercise

Directions: Before you can adopt a more positive outlook, you must make room for positive input. Your circuits can become overloaded with negativity, and they must be cleared for incoming messages of gratitude, optimism, and encouragement. The following visualization exercise, recommended by Philip H. Friedman, is a must if you often feel victimized or negative.

Before starting this exercise, find a comfortable place with no interruptions. Sit in a comfortable chair and take a few minutes just to relax.

Now close your eyes, take a deep breath, and let it out slowly. Relax each muscle group beginning with your toes and slowly move up to your face. When you feel very relaxed, especially all your face muscles, visualize a hot-air balloon that is attached not to the customary basket but to a large garbage can. The balloon is tethered to the ground for the moment. Imagine yourself walking over to the garbage can, lifting the lid off and dumping all your emotional garbage into it. Toss in your negative attitudes, injustices, and resentments. Also, throw away your self-deprecating statements, your helpless and hopeless feelings. Tear off your victim label and remove those blinders and trash them, too.

Now put the lid on tight, untether the balloon and watch it float far away, taking all your victim thoughts, negative feelings, and behaviors with it. Watch it until it is completely gone. Now take a deep breath, let it out slowly and repeat to yourself, "They are *gone.*"

Develop an alternate plan

For example, what if you decide to ask your boss for a smaller raise and he still says no—what then?

Accept the outcome

If you decide that your only solution is to get a part-time job, accept that you are going to have less time to spend on leisure activities.

Conclusion

If you find that your attitude at work is affecting your attitude at home or vice versa, make an effort to separate the two. Don't let negatives at home cause you problems at the office or let problems at the office affect the way you relate to your family.

Chapter 12

10 Steps to a Positive Attitude

Maintaining a positive mental attitude at work is essential to your overall well-being.

Here are 10 tips to help you maintain a positive mental attitude, even when you must work in a negative environment.

1. Keep your life balanced.

If you have a happy home life, when things at work begin to go bad, you can concentrate your efforts on the positive things at home.

2. Don't give up.

We all have setbacks. Don't think of them as an end, but as a beginning.

3. Make the most of the situation.

If things are less than ideal at your job, look for ways to make them more pleasant.

4. Engage in positive self-talk.

Telling yourself you can do something will help you succeed.

5. Visualize success.

This will help make you more self-assured and comfortable in the situation when it occurs.

6. Attack problems head-on.

When a negative situation occurs, find a way to turn it around.

7. Look for the bright side.

Make it a habit to look for the good in life rather than the bad.

8. Maintain a sense of humor.

Don't take yourself too seriously. Look for the humor in daily annoyances.

9. Make work fun.

If you think your job is dull and boring, look for ways to make it more interesting.

10. Accentuate the positives.

Concentrate on ways to use your strengths and abilities and look for ways to improve your weaknesses.

A positive mental attitude can't change a negative work situation into a positive one, but it can help you enjoy the time you spend at work. If you maintain a positive mental attitude, you will be rewarded in all aspects of your life—including success on your job!

> *"What would you attempt to do if you knew you could not fail?"*
>
> —Dr. Robert Schuller

Life-Giving Promise

Post this promise to reinforce your philosophy of achieving a positive mental attitude and healthy self-esteem.

I,_____, being of sound mind, with the determination to live a long, happy, useful, and fulfilling life, do hereby promise to enjoy all the special moments, strive to be my best, look for the opportunities, and accept all the responsibilities of my life.

I know there will be ups and downs, but I will use adversity to grow stronger, to turn negatives into positives and to become all that I can be.

I will assist and guide others on their journey, which enriches mine.

_____   _____
Signature   Date

Index